RUSSIAN POETRY

A Personal Anthology

Mr. FORD

PALME COMMISSION, STOCKHOLM 1982

RUSSIAN POETRY

A Personal Anthology

Selected & Translated

R.A.D. Ford

Drawings by Sharon Katz

mosaic press

Canadian Cataloguing in Publication Data

Main entry under title:
Russian poetry: a personal anthology

ISBN 0-88962-267-1 (PB) ISBN 0-88962-268-X (HC)

1. Russian poetry - 20th century - Translation into English. 2.English poetry -
20th century - Translations from Russian. I. Ford, R.A.D., 1915-

PG3237.E5R87   1984   891.71'4'08   C84-099433-8

Published by Mosaic Press, offices and warehouse at 1252 Speers Road, Units 1
and 2, Oakville, Ontario, L6L 5N9, Canada and Mosaic Press, PMB 145, 4500
Witmer Industrial Estates, Niagara Falls, NY, 14305-1386, U.S.A.

Mosaic Press acknowledges the assistance of the Canada Council and the
Department of Canadian Heritage, Government of Canada for their support of
our publishing programme.

Printed and Bound in Canada

MOSAIC PRESS CANADA:
1252 Speers Road, Units 1 & 2,
Oakville, Ontario, L6L 5N9
Canada
Ph/Fax: 905-825-2130
editorial:
cp507@freenet.toronto.on.ca
orders & service:
mosaicpress@on.aibn.com

MOSAIC PRESS U.S.A.:
PMB 145
4500 Witmer Industrial Estates
Niagara Falls, NY, 14305-1386
U.S.A.
Ph/Fax: 1-800-387-8992
editorial:
cp507@freenet.toronto.on.ca
orders & service:
mosaicpress@on.aibn.com

IN
MEMORIAM
THEREZA

BORIS PASTERNAK

CONTENTS

ANNA AKHMATOVA

OSIP MANDELSHTAM

Through the snow, answering hopes,
registered in truck-drivers' taverns,
Herod, dog-catcher, came with a sack
and an apologetic giggle.

MARINA TSVETAYEVA

INTRODUCTION

English is the language of poetry above any other. The fact that it is also the language of sport and business attests to the genius of the language. There are magnificent poems in other languages, of course, but the vast bulk and richness of poetry in English is incomparable.

Russian, although highly inflected and very difficult, is probably the second language of poetry and has a curious affinity to English verse. Like English it has a vast vocabulary, has painlessly incorporated words from other languages, and has the same suppleness. In French, for example, the language demands precision and its clarity results in beautiful poems. But a French sentence should be constructed in a logical way which often tends to deprive the poem of the element of mystery. English and Russian, however, can be bent and twisted in ways which permit enormous inventiveness. There is only one way in which Russian differs greatly from English verse and that is the ease of rhyme in the former.

Modern Russian poetry dates effectively only from the early 18th century. It is therefore no older than the poetry written in English in the United States and Canada. And it was formed much as North American poetry was, in the context of an expanding, pioneering society. Four of the largest cities in Russia, Leningrad, Odessa, Novosibirsk and Khabarovsk, for example, are younger by far than Montréal and Québec, Boston and New York.

Out of this relatively brief span has come a beautiful and vigorous corpus of poetry, accompanying the great prose of the Russian novelists and thinkers of the 19th and early 20th centuries. But for most people Russian poetry has to be accepted on the word of those who know the language, because even the best translations often fail to do it justice. I have frequently had to reassure friends that Pushkin is a great poet because in translation it is almost impossible to reproduce the tremendous beat, rhyme and rhythm of his lines.

Nevertheless Russian is easier to translate into English, keeping the feel of the original, than into other European languages, as English poetry fits superbly into Russian. There is nothing comparable in any other language to Pasternak's marvelous translations of Shakespeare.

If one looks at the poetry of our century it is perfectly justifiable to put in the same category as Yeats, Eliot, Pound, Auden, Rilke, Garcia Lorca, Claudel, Valéry and Apollinaire such Russian poets as Akhmatova, Tsvetayeva, Pasternak, Mandelshtam and Essenin. It is very hard to bridge the linguistic gap but even the few glimpses English translations give are sufficient to light up the glory of these and other Russian poets of our century.

I have called this selection a personal anthology. From my first days in Russia in 1946, through the difficult last years of Stalin, and the renaissance of young poets in the sixties, I have had a feeling of empathy with Russian poetry. And it is a remarkably accurate way of understanding the Russian character. Poetry is a part of the average Russian in a way a non-Slav finds it hard to accept. Where else can a group of young poets pack 16,000 people into a hockey arena for a recital of their verse and have all of them hanging on every word. Where else can you find taxi-drivers prepared to recite Mayakovsky to you? Where else that a Deputy Minister of Energy is ready and willing to discuss the merits and flaws in the poetry of Blok? Or, as Mandelshtam put it: "Russia is the only place where poetry is really important. They'll kill people for it here."

My job in the many years I spent as a diplomat in Russia was political. But my interest in Russian poetry and my efforts at translations were passports to understanding. My love of their poetry made my unmistakable distaste for the system somehow acceptable.

My selection is indeed very personal. I have not attempted any of the 19th century and few of the modern classics, except for a few poems which particularly appealed to me. There are important modern omissions such as Victor Sosnora, Evgenny Vinokurov, Margarita Aligher and Olga Bergoltz. And I have included a great deal of Andrei Voznesensky. In this case, because he is one of the best modern poets in any language, and he became a friend to me and guide to his own poetry and that of his contemporaries.

Evtushenko once said that "poetry translation is like a woman. If it's beautiful it's not faithful and if it's faithful it's not beautiful." I do not claim my translations meet either desiderata. But if they contribute in even a small way in leading the English-speaking reader to recognize the great treasure of poetry that lies half-hidden behind what to most people is the impenetrability of the Russian language, I will feel the effort was worthwhile.

R.A.D. FORD

BELLA AKHMADULINA

RECOLLECTIONS OF SIBERIA

You say — one shouldn't weep.
Indeed perhaps one shouldn't
Weep — into cold rivers seek
To plunge. One should strive

To survive in dark waters,
Escaping through one's fingers,
Give one's self the rare liberty
Of that other distant shore.

And not in vain I sweetly
Longed for Siberia, that far
Land where secretly and meekly
I saw before me the flowers fade.

How can I find a way to tell
You what was happening to me?
Memory has cast a silvery
Glow on everything.

Baikal's deep and secret waters —
And through its slow moving stream
The omul swims spreading
To the light its glittering plumes.

And those huts, and wooden sheds
half-hidden on the banks,
and brightly coloured locusts
quickly dying in my hand.

And white-striped miracle and wonder —
the chipmunk shoots up suddenly,
with a sharp and secret air
fixing his gaze on me.

I was tempted and I was tortured
by the depth of those running streams.
Cut like diamonds, the water of the Kizil,
and like fire, cold and clean.

But I remember most of all
back there, in the fields of rye,
never did I need to utter
even once a lie.

GOD

Because the girl Nastasia
worked as a char for the old man,
and ran barefoot in foul weather
to fetch vodka for his gullet —

She had a right to a beautiful god,
in a chamber flooded with sun,
dandified, elegant, and just,
in a suit of cloth of gold.

But with the sound of drunken
hiccups, in the midst of misery,
the two blackened icons
did not look like him at all.

Yet, suddenly, plants blossomed,
the pearls turned pink, and,
like a church chorus, the simple
name of her betrothed rang out.

And he rose up by the fence,
presented her with a yellow locket,
and so was taken for a god
in all his youthful grandeur.

And in her heart was holiness,
because of a lilting song,
and wine, because of much sweet-talk,
and because of a blue shirt.

But, even then he looked deceitful,
as he took off her gauze scarf,
and at a near-by barn
caressed her weak shoulders...

And Nastasia combed her hair,
took the scarf by both ends,
and Nastasia sang and wailed,
burying her face in her hands.

"Ah, what have you done to me,
what trouble have you brought!
Why last Monday did you make me
a present of a white rose?

Ah, willow, willow, my willow,
do not wither, willow, wait a little.
What has become of my belief?
only a cross on my breast is left."

And the rain gave place to sun,
and nothing much was happening,
and God was laughing at the girl,
and he did not exist at all.

ANNA AKHMATOVA

SUCH DAYS AS THESE

Such days as these there are before the spring:
When the meadow rests under the heavy snow,
The bare trees shiver happily,
And the warm wind comes tenderly and low.

And your body marvels at its lightness,
And your own home you hardly recognize.
We sing with emotion, and the old melodies
Float up like new songs to the skies.

POEM

The twenty-first. Night. Monday.
The outlines of the capital through the mists.
Why should some idler have invented
That love really exists.

And from laziness, or boredom,
Everyone believed it, and thus they live:
We wait for meetings, fear partings,
And sing songs of love.

But some have discovered the mystery,
And silence has enveloped them...
I came upon it unexpectedly
And have been as if ill since then.

PAVLOVSK

Hilly Pavlovsk still I can see before me,
The round meadow, the lifeless, the very
Darkest, tired and shadowy water.
I can never forget it.

When you pass through its iron portals,
Your body shivers with bliss,
You do not live, you exult, you dream,
And your whole life is transformed.

In the late fall, fresh and sharp
The wind comes happily, alone.
The black firs touched with hoarfrost
Stand up in the half-thawing snow.

Filled with a strange delirium
A dear voice, like a song, resounds.
And on a statue's copper shoulders
Sits a rosy-breasted bird.

DON'T FRIGHTEN ME

Don't frighten me with a terrible fate
And the vast weariness of the north.
To-day is my first anniversary with you,
And this holiday means — separation!
It doesn't matter if we do not meet the dawn,
If the moon does not linger over us.
To-day I will shower you with gifts
Never seen in the world before:
Reflections of me in the water of an
Evening stream, dancing drunkenly,
A glance at the swooning stars which
Cannot halt their fall from heaven:
The echo of my exhausted voice,
Once so fresh and summer-like —
May they help you without pain to hear
The Moscow crows as they weave through the air;
May they turn the gloomy dampness of October
Into the sweetness of a day in May —
Oh, my angel, remember me, remember
When the first snow-flakes begin to fall.

SERGEI ESSENIN

THE GOLDEN GROVE

Suddenly the golden grove stopped
Talking, and in the breathless silence
Of the birches we could feel the cranes
In sad flight overhead, indifferent
To all of us in the autumn days.

Why should they be? We are all
Pilgrims in the world — The hempfield
And the broad moon over the blue lake
Dream of the past, and I stand alone
On the steppe, thinking of my happy youth,

Regretting nothing I have ever done,
The years spent in vain, nor the lilac
Blossom in my heart. The cranes
Are carried out of sight by the wind,
And in the garden the fire

Of bright red mountain ash
Is burning. But it cannot warm us.
The tassels of the ash will never burn.
And the grass, though brown, never die.
Like a tree that sadly drops its leaves,

I drop sad words, scattered
By the wind. And if time should
Gather them unwanted and unneeded...
So be it... The golden grove...
Talking in soft undertones.

BLUE MIST

Blue mist. Snow plenitude.
Transparent lemon-coloured moon.
My heart is touched with silent pain —
Remembering my early years.

The snow by the porch is like quick sand.
Once, under such a moon, without a word,
Drawing my fur cap low on my brow,
Secretly I left my father's house.

I have returned to my own country.
Who remembers me? who has forgotten?
I stand sadly, like a hunted stranger —
Now master of my own domain.

Silently I twist my new hat in my hands,
But the sable means nothing to my soul.
I remember grandfather, I remember grandmother,
I remember the soft cemetery snow.

All are at rest. We will all be there,
It matters nothing if we care or not —
That is the reason why I long for people,
That is the reason why I love people.

That is the reason why I am almost weeping,
And, smiling, I put out my soul —
As if for the last time seeing
This house and the dog on the porch.

DO YOU NOT LOVE ME

Do you not love me, do you not pity me,
Am I so ugly then? Without a glance
At me you faint with passion, dropping
On my shoulder your fair hands.

You are still young with your sensuous smile,
And I to you am neither tender nor rude.
Tell me, how many men have you caressed? How
Many hands do you remember? How many lips?

I know — they passed like shadows
Through your fire, and left no sign.
You have sat on many knees,
As you are sitting now on mine.

What does it matter if you half close
Your eyes and think of some-one else.
As for me, I do not like you very much,
Being sunk deep in the dear past.

Do not call this ardour fate; the
Passionate ties are never true.
As by chance we smiling met,
Quietly I will part from you.

And you will go your way, scattering
Joyless days. Only, touch not with fire
Those who have never kissed, nor those
Who have never felt desire.

And when, chattering about love, you
Stroll with some other man in the street,
Perhaps I too will take a walk
And once again we two will meet.

Moving closer to the other man, bending
Slightly down, with emphasis
You will say quietly: "Good evening,"
And I will answer: "Good evening, miss."

And nothing will trouble my soul,
And nothing excite it again, —
Who has loved once, can love no more,
And who is burned out, is touched in vain.

LETTER TO MY MOTHER

Are you still living, my darling?
I am alive too! And in the night
Send greetings! May your little hut be bathed
In the ineffable evening light.

They write to me that, hiding your
Fear, you grieve deeply about me,
And in your old-fashioned winter coat
Go often to the highway anxiously.

And always in the blue dusk of evening
You see the same vision of my life —
That some one in a tavern brawl
Has stuck in my heart a Finnish knife.

It's all right, my dear! Don't worry.
It is only a bad dream. Who
Would be such a bitter drunkard
To die without seeing you?

I feel for you as tenderly as always,
And from my mutinous sadness rouse
Up to dream of escaping quickly
Back to our lowly house.

I will come back when our white garden
Spreads its branches like the Spring; though
You must not wake me up at dawn
As you did eight years ago.

Do not waken the dreams which are faded,
Nor trouble my old distress —
In my short life I have suffered
Too early a loss and weariness.

And teach me not to pray. I cannot!
To the old times there is no return, no respite.
You are my only help and happiness.
You are my one ineffable light.

So forget now all your troubles,
And don't grieve so much for me.
In your old-fashioned winter coat
Don't go to the highway longingly.

THE SLEIGH

Oh! my sleigh and my fast horse!
You are the devil's work below.
And in the vastness of the steppe
The sleigh-bells laugh, and tears flow.

There is no moon, no barking dog,
In the vast and empty space.
But wait a bit, brave life,
I have not yet left the race.

The night is bad, but sing, coachman,
And I too will join the song —
About the crafty eyes of a girl,
About my gay youth, so long

Ago. Ah! that was the time, when
Happily I would harness my horse,
Put some straw in the sleigh,
And drive off on a wild course.

And in the midnight silence
(God knows where I learned such ways)
My talkative accordion
Persuaded many a maid.

Now all has passed. My hair is thin.
The horse is dead. There is not a noise
In the yard. And, having no chance
To talk, my accordion has lost its voice.

But yet the cold has not touched
My soul. I like the frost and the snow,
Because the sleigh-bells are laughing
Still, at all that happened long ago.

ALL TOO SOON

All too soon we will depart
For the land of peace, that blessed abode.
Perhaps I too will need to gather
Up my frail baggage for the road.

Treasured birch trees of
My soil! My lowlands wide.
And the host of things I'm leaving
With regret I cannot hide.

In this world too much I've loved
The wraith that clothes in flesh the soul.
Peace to the aspens, arms outspread,
Mirrored in the stream below.

Much in silence I have thought,
Many songs myself bequeathed.
And in this grim world I'm glad
That I have lived and breathed.

* * *

I know in that other country
There are no fields golden in the haze.
That is why I cherish those who have
Spent on earth with me their days.

EVGENNY EVTUSHENKO

A STREETCAR NAMED POETRY

I entered the streetcar of poetry
        (like a social welfare office —
full of people and papers)
not through the front entrance,
but hanging on the step.
I balanced adroitly on the buffer
with my hand
      on the door,
and when at last I slipped inside —
I could not believe myself.
I always made way for the old people.
Never hid from the ticket-collector.
Never trod on any-one's toe.
And when they stepped on mine —
       I never complained.
Somebody forced his way into the tram, as if it were paradise
full of his worst enemies,
changing the mob logic of those inside.
Passengers grumbled morosely,
    burying their noses in their papers,
like brood-hens in corn.
"The tram's not made of rubber...
      Stop knocking!
Don't open the door, conductor."
I am with those
      who have come to build and sweep,
not with those
      who say: "No admittance."
I am with those
      who want to get inside the tram
when they are not permitted.
This world is hard, like Moscow in winter,
when the snow blows through its streets.
Trams are made of rubber.
      There are seats!
Open the door,
   conductor!

THE CEMETERY OF THE WHALES

In the cemetery of the whales
        in the snow-covered churchyard

Stand, in place of crosses,
        their own bones.

No use for teeth —
        all teeth are too soft,

No use for soup —
        all pots are too shallow.

Vainly the snow-storm flails,
        but they survive —

As if hammered out of ice,
        like black rainbows.

Hunch-backed Eskimos,
        longing for a shot of vodka,

As if it were a question,
        or a question mark in brackets.

Here comes the camera-man
        Curb that photo passion,

Let the whales rest in peace,
        at least after their death.

Those that lived
        never hurt people,

With childish simplicity
        worshipped fountains.

And the red ball of the sun
        danced in the white foam...

"Whales ahoy! Fire!
        Come on, guys, kill 'em!"

Nowhere to hide?
        You are larger than space.

Nowhere to dive?
        Not enough water in the world.

You think you are God?
        A dangerous vanity,

A harpoon in your flank
        is payment for your grandeur.

Greatness makes everyone
        hunt for it.

He is a fool who is great.
        Smaller is smarter.

Cockroaches are like noodles.
        Nothingness

Makes helpless majesty
        a challenge for teasing.

Hands holding the field-glasses are shaking
        with excitement, aiming,

And with a harpoon in his side
        Tolstoy flees from "Zeiss".

Shoals frighten majesty.
        Rafts are broken up on the rocks.

In the remains of harpoons
        Gorky's cast ashore,

Hemingway is silent,
        but on his tomb sternly

The harpoon sticks out of the grass
 up from the coffin.

And hidden by the crowd
 the cowboy from Dallas

With telescopic sights
 does his bloody job.

... The hunt goes on,
 and after death, kindness.

Honest are your laws,
 cruel Alaska.

No hypocritical flowers lie
 on the ice-floes

In the cemetery of whales.
 The Eskimos have tact.

Oh, hunch-backed Eskimo —
 The white man has his ways:

After firing the harpoon
 they cry over the prey.

They mourn more modestly than virgins,
 tears on their cheeks.

The murderers draped in black,
 form the honour guard.

And the hunters,
 for whom no place is here

Carry wreaths
 on behalf of Centralharpoontrust.

But the flowers are tied up
 with harpoon wire.

I've had enough kindness.
 Let me go to the Eskimos.

AT FORTY

When forty years come round
it's time to ask oneself:
is the soul not sick at heart? —
faced with his forty years
and with every drop of milk
and with every crumb of bread.

When forty years come round
no excuses can be made,
either to God or to oneself.
All those tears one caused
all that drivel written
come back to rest.

When forty years come round
it's time to call a halt
to the thirst for pleasure:
perhaps flesh should be suppressed,
and if flesh licks its lips,
it means it consumed the soul.

Well, when one is consumed
by lips, like an antichrist,
this is the end of flesh.
One affair, another affair,
and in the end — only mist and naked
women, like a Turkish bath.

Up to forty the aim is clear.
Up to forty all life is a spree.
But at forty — it's just a hangover.
The head is thick.
The words are blurred.
Like a house-warming in a gutter.

Before forty, before forty
we march to the fair and we'll
seize luck by the horns,
but at forty, quietly, by foot,
drag ourselves home with an empty sack.
We have been robbed — and we weep.

When forty years come round,
he should take his own advice:
stay away from fairs.
That's how it's done — no cheating: no deal.
And if you cheat you become a cheat yourself.
That is the law of the deal.

But it's worse to see a horse
neighing and trembling
in the hands of a dealer, a fleecer.
The shame is much the same —
when you sell something and when
somebody sells you.

When forty years come round,
life is painted in grey,
but if you can't be chestnut
then be dapple-grey
and don't sell a scrap of your
dappled skin on market day.

When forty years come round,
life looms larger
than the bustle of a country fair.
Everything is ahead — and you wait for it.
Don't fall into comedy,
but don't get lost in tragedy.

When forty years come round,
it's either boom — or bust —
man himself decides.
He cannot save himself from death,
but nothing, except death,
can stop him flourishing.

JOHN REED'S MONOLOGUE

I am John Reed
    I am buried beside
        the red Kremlin wall.
That grey crypt, Wall Street,
        does this jar on you?
Neither a Broadway fop
      nor a scribbler
        from "The Masses",
I, like a peon,
      walked together with you, rebellious Mexico.
And when at last
      you, Russia, shouted "Aurora",
I, educated in Harvard,
      was going to capture the Winter Palace!
I was looking for a hope,
      I climbed to the tops of mountains
        and rolled down,
I drank heady pepper vodka —
      cactus home-brew.
Harvard, do not judge me too severely
      if I, brought up in the best circles
        from my youth,
guzzled cabbage soup with sailors
      in the canteen of seething Smolny.
I saw with my watchful eyes
      how the revolution was stained at times,
but I loved Pancho who was as pure as Chapaev.
And in the eyes of muzhiks
      who frightened you so much,
        bread-and-butter-lily-white ladies,
I saw Lenin
      even before I met
        Lenin.

FEAR
(Extracts)

In Russia fear is dying now
Like the ghosts of olden times, though
Begging still for bread with the old
Women huddled in church doors.

I recall them, powerful and strong,
At the court of triumphant lies.
Fear floated like a shadow everywhere,
Penetrating every floor.

That day has gone, far away, and now
It is hard even to recall
The secret fear of someone's curse,
Or of a knock upon the door.

We were not afraid of work or weather
Or of fighting at the front,
But sometimes we felt a deadly fear
Of speaking even to ourselves.

Now fear is dying in Russia,
And, well, things are not so bad.
Buildings are going up without fear,
And they are real, and not imagined.

We were not defeated or dishonoured.
And in her enemies Russia,
Which conquered fear, now creates
An even greater fright.

Happily now I look and see
New fears: of being untrue to the land,
Fear of lies, destroying truth, and
Turning truth itself into lies.

Fear of boasting, of stupidity,
Fear of copying another's words,
Fear of destroying with mistrust
And of trusting oneself too much.

Fear of being happy, but indifferent
To another's cares and sorrows
Fear of being timid, cautious
Before the page, the drawing-board.

And so I write these lines,
Perhaps unwittingly too fast,
I write oppressed with fear
I have not given them all my soul.

IVAN KHARABAROV

THE TAIGA

The taiga bore me
    in a dark wood,
One green
   and humid night.
Boughs were stroking
     her face,
An old cedar
    did what it could
To help and for a long
     time she tossed
And moaned with pain.
I was born
    in thickets of sleep and rain,
Merry, stubborn and swart.
I stirred them up,
     spared not my strength,
And my clear voice
     rang out in the air.
And the bears looked
     from their wooded dens
In amazement at me.
With the squirrels
    I played merrily —
Catching pine cones in the air.
On the brink of a precipice I stood still
And greedily gulped down
     emptiness.
Oh, taiga,
    my pine-needled mother
in a soft sable fur,
You are large
    I cannot take you in my arms,
I can only
   kiss you...
I left you, across
     the water, in the spring,
And live far away from you.

At night
               you come to me in my dreams,
Touching my cheek
                    with your needles.
And forever
               I am close to you, I am yours.
Give me vision
                    and pride of your hills,
Let me find what I seek,
                         and follow me
With the eyes
               of your lakes.

SEMION KIRSANOV

SUDDENLY

Suddenly
I am the same age
As you:
I am the champion of bicycling,
Boxing, hiking,
And — everything!

Leaving our footsteps on the sand
For the archaeologists, and the centuries,
We rush to the edge of the tide
And plunge into the ocean.
We decide to cross the strait.
Beside us swims — a vertical
Interrogation mark in the sea,
Or a chessman's knight,
On which you came into the world.
You, dressed only in hair and beads,
Thrust your slight form into the depths.

I, in my aqualung,
Fight off the sharks,
And seek you in the multi-coloured depths.
Oh, how new it is to be
The same age as you.
There is only us
And our underwater love
Among the coral reefs and rocks.
We dive again!
And swim among the fish,
Medusae, needle-fish, and stars!

And your rosy arms in the depths
Are swept like sea-weed
Into mine.
Suddenly
I am the same age
As you.

I AM WHITE, DARLING

I am white,
darling.
I am — chalk
which was sea
and fish and bird
and became white.
I am the era of chalk,
Deep in the sea
the mark of sea-shells on me.
The palm of my hand
is only the imprint of a fossilized leaf.
And you are the beginning.
You — the dragon-fly in flight.
You — the flash of the flying-fish.
You — sky of the first storm.
You — life just beginning.
You — are the rainbow,
the first of the prism.
You — the opening of eyes.
You — waterfall of golden hair.
You — the first flight of early bees.
And I — chalk.
And in my heart
deep down the cliché
of the dragon-fly, and fish, and bird.
And with your happy hand
sundering the stone, the white
of me —
read:
"He loved you."

OSIP MANDELSHTAM

THREE OCTETS

1

I'm coming, coming out of space
Into the forgotten garden of value,
And with the consciousness of reason,
Tear up imaginary constancy.

Alone I read, without people,
Your textbook — infinity —
Savage, leafless medical book,
Manual for enormous roots.

2

The hard crust of nature breaks,
The hard blue eye penetrates its law.
The ores play happily in earth's crust,
And like ore, a hymn breaks from my chest.

Deaf, weak solitary seeks,
As if by the road bent into horn,
To understand all outer space,
Profusion, the petal's voice and the rim of sky.

3

The Tartars, the Uzbeks and the Nentsi,
And the whole Ukrainian nation,
And even the Volga Germans
Expect interpreters now.

And perhaps, at this very moment,
Some Japanese is translating
Me into Turkish, penetrating
Into my very soul.

FINDING A HORSESHOE

What to start with?
Everything cracks and shifts.
The air shivers with comparisons.
Not one word is better than another,
The earth buzzes like a metaphor,
And light carriages
In the abrupt harness of the flight of birds
                      strained by effort
Break into parts,
Trying to compete with the snorting favourites
                      at the hippodrome.

Thrice happy he who puts a name in his song
For the song adorned with a title
Lives longer among other songs —
And the ribbon on his forehead distinguishes him
                      among his friends,
Rescues him from oblivion, from a too strong and
                      enveloping perfume,
Intimacy of man,
Smell of a wild beast,
Or simply the perfume of savory rubbed between the hands.

The air is sometimes dark like water, and every living
                      thing swims in it like fish,
With their fins separating the sphere,
Compact, supple, barely warm,
Crystal where the wheels turn and the horses are reined in,
Humid black earth of Nereus every night turned over
By pitchforks, tridents, hoes, plows.
The air is thick like earth —
It is impossible to get out of it, hard to get in.
From its green bat springs a rustle of leaves;
The children play knucklebones with the vertebrae
                      of dead animals.

The frail chronology of our era is coming to an end.
Thanks for that which has been.
I have been wrong, I have gone astray, I have lost
                      my accounts.
Our era vibrated like a golden ball,

Hollow, moulded, held up by no-one,
At any touch replying: "Yes" or "No",
As a child answers:
"I will give you an apple", or "I won't give you an apple".
And its face is an exact copy of the voice which
                pronounces these words.

The sound rings out again, though the cause of the
                sound has vanished.
The horse lies in the dust and snorts, his mouth foaming,
But the sharp curve of his collar
Retains memory of the race, the legs going in every
                direction,
When they were more than four,
As many as stones on the road,
Stones multiplied by four,
By the trotter, gleaming with the heat, striking the soil.

So,
Whoever finds a horseshoe
Breathes its dust,
And rubs it with a scarf, until it shines,
Then,
Nails it to the door
So it can rest a little,
And never again will have
To tear the star out of the flint.

The lips of man,
              when they have nothing more to say,
Keep the form of the last word said,
And in his hand a feeling of heaviness,
Although the pitcher
           is half emptied,
              on the way home.
What I say now, it is not I who speak,
It was exhumed like fossilized seeds of wheat.
Some strike the form of lions on coins,
Others —
           a head;
Different pieces of copper, gold and bronze
Are equally honoured in the soil.
The century to gnaw them marked them with its teeth.
Time amputates me like a coin,
And already a piece of me is missing.

SAMUEL MARSHAK

IMMORTALITY

Four years
I was immortal.
Four years
I was carefree,
For I did not know that death was coming,
For I did not know life was not eternal.

You, who know how to live in the real present,
Believe not in death, like immortal children.
That moment is always for to-morrow,
Though death may be even now at hand.

VLADIMIR MAYAKOVSKY

CRIMEA

When I walk, or look from my window —
flowers, and the blue sky —
magnolia bursts under my nose,
glazinia in my eye.

For milk I exchanged tea.
In the charm of moonlight,
by day, by night, in Chaeer
water runs, roaring.

Under the dreadful eye of the struggling waves,
trytons and naiads,
cast out of the palaces,
decay in the deep waters.

And in the palaces there is new life:
having tasted watery pleasures,
go, worker, and lie down
on the bed of Grand Dukes.

The mountain-anvils are aflame
and the sea is a blue blouse.
The repairs of the people are quick
in the huge Crimean forge.

LAST PAGE OF THE CIVIL WAR

Glory to you, red star hero.
Having washed the earth with blood,
for the glory of the Commune,
from mountain to mountain-top
through the Crimean fortress.
Their tanks crawled over the trenches,
the muzzles of their guns protruding;
you filled the trenches with your bodies,
and crossed the isthmus over the dead.
They dug their lines of trenches,
they whipped with lead the river,
and you took from them Perikop
almost with your bare hands.
You did not only conquer the Crimea,
and defeat the white battalions.
The blow was twofold:
you won with it
the great right to labor.
And if a sunny life should come
after the days of gloom,
we know you won it by your bravery
in the Perikop attack.
All words are joined in thanks to you,
red star lava.
For centuries and centuries, comrades,
for you
glory, glory, glory!

BULAT OKUDZHAVA

NOT ABOUT DEATH

To die —
means also knowing how
to choose taut sails
for the meeting with the sky.
Good, if you choose yourself,
worse, if others help you.
To die —
means also knowing how
to live
and not confuse the flash
of recognition
with the smile of slander,
and to have time
to put that penultimate touch
on the picture,
the penultimate rhyme.
To die —
means also knowing how,
no matter what constant, stubborn
knocks one's life deals out...
To seek absolution?
What a little thing for
the happiness of eternity.
What? Sins?
The poems remain.
And their outrage at the world goes on,
asking no indulgences.
If there were sins... perhaps,
but there are no sins...
There is only motion.

RUISPIRI — A COMIC BALLAD

The beauty of red bark.
The tiles of roofs.
The scab of moss.
And the Gambori heights,
Sprinkled with the blood of hawks.
Everything is so simple!

The shadows at sunset are quiet.
In the tavern of Ruispiri
the tavern-keeper,
a happy trickster,
downing his tenth glass,
glorifies my sins.

I do not shrink from wine,
I am not squeamish.
He laughs:
he has no faith in me when I am sober,
and wants no talk
without something flowing.

I drink so and so,
on an empty stomach,
clumsily and badly...
(I am, perhaps, half a century behind
the nearest scribblers.)
Resting his back against the millstones
he seems to be teasing me.

I teach him sober words,
he teaches me idleness.
I try to quiet him down,
as I can,
urge him to be
more sensible...
He teaches me to live merrily
and laughs,
opening his bottomless mouth.

Ten barrels are empty.
                    I am not drunk.

But it may turn out badly yet!...
He is having his two hundredth glass
to my eloquence:
"God bless you!..."
Twenty barrels lie in the yard
quite empty.
In the glow of evening
our relations are quite simple.
Forty barrels lie in the yard.
And it is we who have emptied them
in the glow of evening,
on the outskirts of the village of Ruispiri!

Everything is just right in this land,
like paradise!
Isn't it what we are looking for?
I get to know myself,
for the air is cleansed here.
All my words are left behind,
                    in the cities,
forgotten.
All my mistakes,
like windows in old houses,
are boarded up,
All caprices
(there are whole heaps of them,
like piles of unwashed dishes,
there).

Somewhere there,
holding his peace,
great though lived out,
my last beloved bigot
cannot reach me.

No earth.
The whole earth is between the skies and me.
The rest is
a mere trifle.
And the last Alpine flower
            that has not felt the heat
despises our tearful verses...

BORIS PASTERNAK

INDIAN SUMMER

The currant bushes, the leaves of the currant
Bushes are crudely made. In the house
They are crushing the berries, making
Home-brew, kvass, putting cloves
In the pickles. There is a sudden
Guffaw, and the glasses tinkle.

Scornfully, the woods retreat away
From the noise, up the steep slope,
Where the hazels burn in the sun as if
Singed by the heat of camp-fires.

Here the road descends into the ravine,
Through the twisted trunks of trees,
And all, alas, the trees, the grove
And the rag-man autumn
Are swept into the gully.

Well, after all, does anything really matter?
Is the world easier than all
The scholars think? The copse
Is half drowned in the swamp water,
And to each in his time comes an end.

Listen without understanding, senselessly,
When everything before you is aflame!
And the white autumnal ash is drawn
Like a web across the window pane.

Go out of the garden through the gap
In the fence, and disappear somehow
Into the birch grove. In the house —
Laughter and the sounds of cooking.
And in the distance — the same noise,
And the same laughter.

WHITE NIGHT

Far in the past, dimly it comes back to me,
A house on the Petersburg quay,
You — a student, from Kursk, daughter
Of a poor merchant from the steppes.

You were lovely, with so many admirers,
Both of us were beautiful that white night,
We found a place on your window-sill
And looked down on your far sky-scrapers.

The morning touched with the first
Tremor the street lamps, like
Butterflies of gas. So, quietly, I talked
To you as if you were asleep.

We embraced, we kissed, and I
Felt shy with the true secret,
As the panorama of Petersburg, from
The Neva banks spread out before us.

There, far off in the misty distance
Of this night of Spring-like whiteness,
The nightingales with glorious thunder
Announced the frontiers of Summer.

With crazy abandon, traffic roared through
The streets. The voice of a little bird
Far off awakened rapture and confusion
In the depths of a charmed thicket.

Disguised as a barefoot wanderer
The night slipped along the garden fence,
And left on our windowsill the trace
Of a conversation overheard.

In the echoes of an overheard conversation,
In the garden, in the startled shadows,

The branches of the apple and cherry trees
Were decked out in the colour of whitewash.

And the trees, white ghosts, pressed
Like a multitude into the street,
The signs of farewell of the white
Nights... having seen so much.

THE WIND

I have come to my end, but you
Are living still, and the wind, complaining
And weeping, shakes the forest
And the cottage, not each pine-tree
Separately, but the whole wood,
And with the whole boundless distance
The sailboats moving on the gleaming
Surface of the harbour —
Not from boldness, nor from aimless
Anger, but in yearning rather, seeking
Words for your lullaby.

ROBERT ROZHDESTVENSKY

IN THE NIGHT

How silent is the world,
how warm!...
But if you, —
in this silence,
to
   spite
       me,
and to spite
          yourself —
grow tired
of thinking about me.
And on an impulse
          dial a number
and silently
fling wide the door...
Maybe, I
      don't even know
him,
who is standing at the door.
And even if I know him,
             all right...
He is
    considerate.
He has
    a soul...
And now
you come
      to
         his
arms.
Trembling and pale.
And nothing do you understand.
And the sheets are like
          thin smoke...
And in the oblivion
        that falls
          on you

call him
by my own
name!
And you are falling, half alive,
and you are choked
                with tears.
And you are whispering
                ardent
                    words.

Those words.
Those very words.
In earnest...
The twilight
            seems on fire
And your head
aflame...
The telephone girl:
"Hello
Whom should I call
                in Moscow?..."
"Whoever answers..."
Maybe,
        you.
But if it is him,
             well, then...
Then let
your telephone number be
crossed out for good!...
And out of the dusk
a slow pain
          approaches
              me.
But now I laugh
          at it!
It's funny,
like this
      I quarrel
with you
and then again
          make peace.

My thoughts,
I try to calm them
down —
      waiting for the storm to break...
And how long
      the phone
           keeps still!
How loud
the ticking
of the clock!

KONSTANTIN SIMONOV

DEATH STRUCK HIM

Death struck him like a bullet, silent,
Sudden, and he lies pale — already nothing.
And the honour guard of four, young
No longer, stands at attention.

Four, unbelievers, accompanying once
And forever the fifth on his last road,
Knowing they never again will meet.

And in their eyes — a resolution,
As if they thought he could still
Be saved, as if they could lift him on
Their shoulders and bear him from the fray.

MARINA TSVETAYEVA

POEM

When I look at the falling leaves
Drifting down to the cobble-stones,
Swept away — as if by the brush of an
Artist finally finishing a picture,

I think (already no-one likes the way
I stand, or my pensive glance),
How a truly yellow, really rusty leaf
Has been forgotten up there.

GARDEN

For this hell,
For this delight,
Give me a garden
For my dying years.

In my dying years,
In my troubled age,
Years of toil,
Years of sweat.

In my awful, aging
Years — give me
Some warm years
And a cool garden.

Fur a fugitive,
Give me a garden:
Without anyone,
Without a soul.

Garden: Not a step!
Garden: Not a glance!
Garden: Not a smile!
Garden: Not a cry!

Without an ear,
Give me a garden.
Without perfume!
Without a soul!

Say: "You've suffered enough —
Take this garden, alone, like you"!
(You too, will not stay!)
"Take this garden, alone, like you".

Such a garden for my dying years!
"This garden? Is it perhaps the other world?"
Give it me for my dying years,
For the absolution of my soul.

ALEXANDER TVARDOVSKY

POEM

The blue snow is turning black
Along the roads leading out of town,
And the water seeps down into
Patches of limpid sand.

Under the apparently immovable
Surface, the stream waits quietly,
And then one rainy night will burst
Unexpectedly from the river-bed.

And the earth, sleepy, melting,
Has hardly dried out when the dead leaves
Meld in the ground, and new grass
Begins to push up through the earth.

And the alder's pollen, drifting
Green and tender on the breeze,
Touches the cheek like a shadow
From distant childhood days.

And once again my heart responds
As in the past to the year's awakening —
Not gone, not finished, but with
You still, and forever more.

ANDREI VOZNESENSKY

THE EDGE

Twilight over the field is blurred,
and the sun, setting beyond the forest,
lights up the edge of the plowed land
so it gleams like a silver rail.

Only a minute, like the sting of a bee,
will that secret beauty last.
But every evening I go to see
how the sliver of light fades away.

My early evening love,
my love, my farewell love,
a golden sliver of light
under closing doors.

ANGUISH

Glancing at the train from hills touched with autumn,
or straying into an evening village —
my soul feels
              sucked out by a pump,
as if it were drawn out, dampened down,
as if something had happened or were about to happen —
the collar-bones, below the throat, sucked out.

Or is it some neglected guilt aching?
Or did I make a woman unhappy and this is my punishment?
Putting a song together, I feel remitted,
              but later the pain grows worse.
The road has been shown, but the way forbidden...

I am worn out by a secret tumor in my breast —
and the pain overwhelms me.

I have forgotten what your hair is like.
I have forgotten what your breath is like.
Grant me forgiveness if I am to blame.
And, absolving me, give back my guilt again.

FORGIVE ME!

From the dry, rattle-like dahlias,
And perhaps too in my sleep —
I hear the echo of a trite phrase: forgive me,
For some reason addressed to me.

Some line must have stuck in
The audio-archive of my memory.
I've never been to America. Why "forgive me"?
Why torture me in this un-Russian way?

As if the soul, like a repentant jokester,
Departs, discarding you like underwear.
As if you, the master, torment your
Dog, and then beg its pardon.

But there must be some-one to blame
For those years that were killed,
The flesh and blood sold for a kopek.
And I repeat again and again: forgive me —
My own sigh, addressed to myself.

FOR A PORTRAIT OF ANNETTE VALLON

I write you from Wordsworth's cottage
not to boast — from idiocy,
that I am not with you under the damp hair
of centuries, leaning against the fence.

You, perhaps, will correct my "Wordsworth",
but it doesn't matter — I am not with you,
at least on you it would be more like sea-weed.
Like spread toes — like water-lilies on a pond.

About the future don't think. About the past
don't grieve. Look, because of Wordsworth
there exists a hamlet on the map,
rows of birches, coated with phosphorous,
the irreparableness of a mountain vista,
or lakes — like the echo of his lament
about Anne and that which cannot be repaired.

Grasmere, 18 November, 1981

WHY

Why do lampreys swim from Riga back
To Canadian shores, the land of their ancestors?
Why rename streets?
Build new ones, with new names.

People once lived in them and each was wonderful.
What if they come, remembering the Neva?
I will never forget you.
Or, rather, temporarily, as long as I live.

RECOMMENDATION

Night and evening, morning, every day
I give thanks I died not yesterday.

The bullet of the enemy struck the candle,
I give thanks for the holy rites.
The foe on your back more desired than your brother,
I give thanks I died not yesterday.

I give thanks I died not yesterday,
and grateful in my garden and house with its old terrace
I died not yesterday and grateful
for the crab-apple in bloom this morning.

And you, will never come into my life
like a blonde and sinful force,
pure, as if you had remitted my sins
and illuminated my life — quite miraculous.

Never would know if you were fresh in the morning,
if another man would wake you up,
That would be — incomprehensible!
I give thanks I died not yesterday.

The loss is terrible. The lots are drawn.
Accept one's fate, without a word.
Like Brummel, one must start from scratch.
I give thanks I died not yesterday.

Existence — it would be a sister
if we made not magic errors.
Life — it is like love, thus
I give thanks I died not yesterday.

It is the miracle which is right, not hatred.
Perhaps tomorrow one will say — "Time!"
So, scratch with a smiling pen:
"I give thanks I died not yesterday."

AUTUMN PRELUDE

Untie my tongue, Muse of fiery ABC.
It's time to test the roar.
Untie my tongue,
                 as you untie the elms
at the fall of the leaf,

as, sniffing in the wind,
at the mosses under the arms of the bare birches,
the wild boars howl.
It means, autumn is here in earnest.

Release my tongue from idle talk,
from the standard ligatures,
and not in the way castor oil cleanses my colleagues,
untie me my tongue.

Refresh my tongue, modern Muse.
Having filled your mouth with vodka from the fridge,
you gave me it tickling, frosty, neat!
The taste of rowanberry and a Russian dictionary.

I threw the dumbfounded audiences at your feet by dozens,
leaving them stuttering.
Like a desperate girl,
                       my windpipes were tied.
Deliver me of the word. Untie me my tongue.

And nobody knew how, in the strain of emotion,
I tore myself to shreds — and you thought I was crazy?
I thought — what if they recover from the shock!
Untie me my tongue.

Time of the roar of the beast, of the chamois' moulting.
Blasting the Adam's apple with an archaic howl,
not the Latin "August", but the ancient "Roar",
light up my tongue!

The roar
            of overloaded markets and trucks,
when the beasts howl in sweet alarm,
and the air over the fields quivers, like nostrils,
                    sense change,
when under the storage dam of the Ob Hydro-Electric Station,
                    like an exhibit under glass,
the faded field is preserved, where Kuchum's horde
                    faltered long ago,
the roar
when in the upper left-hand corner of the florid,
                    pearly-white birch,
a squirrel lurks, bright red, like the capital letters
                    of the Chronicle of Ipatiev,
roar,
            oh, let me have a piece of your tune!

History roars. The roar of the bison penetrates the heart.
And bending in tears over the corpse of the Sahara
lions are howling,
            like telephone poles,
                    lifting vertically
                            their bobbed tails,
roar!

The roar of fallen pears
                    and Ministerial Cabinets,
enviably overripe,
the roar of bare country, like leafless trees,
the roar.

The unanimous roar of a family which grabbed a "Moskvich"
                    at the lottery,
why not a "Volga" at one stroke!
Yaroslavna in a skyscraper still doesn't understand herself —
The roar.

The roar of happy meetings,
holiday of new clothes,
a woman's parting roar
at the first good-byes to childhood.

We are tribesmen of the forest.
Changes sing in us.
Something is pressing inside us.
Man roars in chorus.

The cobwebs fly. Space fades away.
From across the river something beckons.
To find your voice, you must part in sorrow,
the roar,
the roar means "Farewell", the roar means
            "Long live tomorrow!"

Like burning oakum, scraps of wolves and dogs stick to the
        thickets.
They are paying taxes for their prophetic howl.
Paying with their hides for a song.
Untie me my tongue.

Over my jacket I have
                a flat with sleeves of corridors,
where from the mailbox,
        like a handkerchief from the pocket, a newspaper
        sticks out,
the top floor, like a boyar's coat
            of stone fur, —
untie me my tongue.

Oh, is my craft original? No, it is self-tormenting!
You beat me against the wall, asleep, awake,
and torture me with routine, until I utter the Word.
Put me on any rack, until I start roaring.

The roar of new words. The roar of ripe premonitions,
revolutions and races.
The roar of the first oven,
twisted in a red glow...
The Virgin Smell of Snow,
which changes you.

Almost human, a squirrel squeals
on the highway. It looks as if it had been
dyed in the Vyatka, already aluminium-coloured,
only its little snout and paws crimson.

PORTRAIT OF PLISETSKAYA

In her very name is a ripple of applause.
It rhymes with weeping larches,
with Persian lilac,
The Champs Elysées, Advent.
There are temperatures, geographic and magnetic poles.
Plisetskaya is the pole of magic.
She twists her audience into the furious cyclone of her thirty-two
fouettés, with her spirit charms, whirls, never lets go.
There are ballerinas of silence, snow-flake ballerinas —
they fade away. She is like a spark from hell.
If she perishes, she will scorch half the planet!
Even her silence is a furious, shouting silence
of expectation, an active and strained silence
between lightning and the thunder-clap.
Plisetskaya is the Tsvetaeva of ballet.
Her rhythm is tight, explosive.

Once upon a time there lived a girl — either Maya or Marina —
it doesn't matter.
Even in childhood her timidity was frightening. The power of her
destiny was visible. She is fed with porridge, with noodle soup,
her hair is braided so tightly it hurts, she practises hand-
writing squeezing her letters obliquely on the paper; a silver
coin she is playing with, its edge glittering, rolls under the
dusty belly of a sideboard.
But she is already tormented by her gift — which is tremendous,
but still for her obscure.

"What shall I do, a first-born and a singer,
Do in a world where the blackest is grey!
Where inspiration is preserved in a Thermos!
Immeasurable in a world of measure?"

Every gesture of Plisetskaya is an ecstatic cry, a dance-question,
an angry reproach:
"What am I to do?"
What is to be done with this "weightlessness in
the world of weights?"

She was born to be weightless.

In a world of heavy, blunt objects.
Aerial in a world of awkwardness.

It seems to me that the décor of "Raymonda", stuffy,
treacly props, the pedestrian staging must infuriate every-one.
She dances desperately alone.
The amazement of genius in the midst of the ordinary —
that is the key to each of her roles.
A surge of blood whirls her around. She is not an ordinary
Aeolian fairy.

"Others there are, with shining eyes and face,
But as for me, I talk with the wind at night.
Not with some young
Italian breeze,
But with the strong, sweeping
Russian gale!"

For the first time in a ballerina something has broken through —
not just feminine graces but a woman's visceral shout.
In "Carmen" for the first time she
walked heavily on the flat of her feet.
Not the points of her toes, but strongly,
carnal, human.

"The glass is full. The glass is empty.
Moon and mud. The guitars are tipsy.
A figure swings to the right, to the left...
A gypsy is a prince. The prince a gypsy."

Fire there is not enough for her in this indecisive world.

"You trained me to live in fire itself.
You thrust me into the snowy steppe!
This, my darling, is what you did to me!
My darling, tell me what I did to you!"

This is the way she loves.
Not for her whisperings, half-measures, compromises.
Playful is her reply to a foreign correspondent:
— What do you hate most?
— Noodles!
And she puts into it not only the tear-stained humiliation
of her childhood.

As an artist everything about her is serious. Well, yes,
naturally, the most disgusting is — noodles; they are a
symbol of standardization, over-cooked spinelessness,
banality, humility, anti-spirituality.
Doesn't she write about "noodles" in her notebook:
"People should defend their convictions...
... with the strength of their spiritual 'ego' alone."
Maya Plisetskaya does not respect noodles!
She is a master.

> "I know that Venus is hand-made.
> Being an artisan, I understand handicraft!"

Ballet rhymes with flight. There are super-sonic flights. A prima
ballerina's furious energy represents the overcoming of the limits
of the body as muscular movement becomes spiritual. Some-one
has spoken about Plisetskaya's exaggerated "technique", about
her withdrawal into "form". Formalists are those who are not
masters of form. Therefore form bothers them and rouses their
envy when they see it in others. They, permanent crammers,
pant over their only rhythm and toil at their twelve fouettés.
Plisetskaya is like a poet lavish and saturated with skill. She is
not a slave to form.
"I am not one of those who behind the thick laurels of success
perceive ninety-five per cent work and five per cent talent."
This is polemical.
I knew a poet who undertook to turn any-one into a poet in
five man-years. And in ten man-years could he make a Pushkin?
He did not make one of himself.

We have forgotten the words "gift", "genius", "inspiration".
Without them art is nothing. As the experiments of
Kolmogorov showed, art cannot be programmed, and two
characteristics of man, his feeling for religion and poetry, cannot
be deduced. Talent cannot be raised by forced growth. It is
born. It is part of the national wealth, like deposits of radium,
September in Sigulda or a medicinal spring.
Plisetskaya's dance is just such a wonder, part of the national
wealth. Art has always been the surmounting of barriers. Man
does not want to express himself in the way predestined by
nature.

Why does man long for the stratosphere? Is there so little to do
on Earth?

The barrier to creativity is being conquered. It is a natural overcoming of nature.

The spiritual path of man is the creation of a new sense organ — the sense of wonder. This is the name for art. The beginning of it is the overcoming of the age-old means of expression.

Every-one walks vertically but man longs to fly horizontally. The public moans with joy when a thirty degree body flies. Stravinsky irritates the eyes with his varied colours. Scriabin experimented with colour by ear. Richter, like a blind man, closing his eyes tight and breathing heavily, gropes for colour through the key-board. The ear becomes an organ of sight. Painting seeks three dimensions and motion on the static canvas. The dance is not only an overcoming of gravity. Ballet is an overcoming of the barrier of sound.

Is the tongue the organ of sound? Or the throat? No, no. Hands and shoulders sing, fingers chirp, conveying something very important for which sound is too crude. Skin thinks and finds its means of expression. Is it a song without words? Music without sound.

There is a fleeting moment in "Romeo" when silence, invisible but tangible, leaves the lips of the youth and floats like a balloon towards Juliet's outstretched fingers.
She takes the materialised sound between her hands, as if it were a vase, and caresses it with her fingers.
The sound is perceived through her touch!
In this the ballet equals love.
Arms speak, ankles think and hands autonomously communicate with each other without intermediaries. The state of sound is occupied by movement. We see sound. Sound is line. Communication is figure. The comparison with Tsvetaeva is not accidental. Plisetskaya has a deep feeling for poetry. I remember her, in black, on a couch, as if she were dissociated from the audience. She sits half-turned and bent like the statue of the girl with the jug in Tsarkoe Selo. Her eyes are closed. She listens with her neck. She is listening with her Modigliani neck, with her skin and the line of her back-bone. Her ear-rings, and her nostrils are quivering.
She likes Toulouse-Lautrec. The biblical lines of the Sevan and Armenia, a bonfire, smoke from a shashlik give her the sensation of summer and rest.

The representative of an elegant magazine visited her once to find out the "rations" of a prima ballerina.
Oh these ethereal elfs and ephemeral sylphs of other times! "My peignoir consists of one drop of Chanel." "The dinner of a ballerina is a rose-petal..."

Plisetskaya's reply is thunderous and Homeric.
Like artists and athletes in the Olympic games.
"I'm starved!"
The intensity is a match for Mayakovsky.
What a humiliating controversy!

I met Plisetskaya in a house where everything spoke of Mayakovsky. From the wall a framed self-portrait of Mayakovsky grinned at us. A woman in grey was clasping her hands. She was speaking about hands in the ballet. I won't repeat all of it. Her hands were moving and swaying near the ceiling, just her hands. Her legs and body were only a vase for those bare, swaying stems. It is dangerous to visit this house. The everlasting and commanding presence of Mayakovsky flattens out the ordinary. Not every-one can stand such a presence. Maya can stand it. She is the most modern of our ballerinas. Our century has poetry, painting, physics but not ballet. This is a ballerina of 20th century rhythms. She is to dance not among swans but among cars and cranes! I see her against a background of Henry Moore's pure lines and the chapel of Rondchamps.
"A genius of pure beauty," in the tense and bustling world.
Beauty purifies the world.
Hence her world-wide fame.

Paris, London, New York lined up for beauty, for tickets to see Plisetskaya. As usual, the world is stunned by an artist who has stunned her own country. It is not only a matter of ballet.
Beauty saves the world. The artist, by creating beauty, transforms the world by creating purifying beauty. In Cuba and in Paris she is equally understood.
Her silhouette resembles an ancient Egyptian painting.
And her name is as short as the name of a girl of our times, in tights, and as thunderous as the name of a goddess or a pagan priestess — Maya.

PUBLIC BEACH No. 2

On ministers, on actors
the sun, with its yellow heel,
like a floor-polisher,
      burns
the people-parquetry

Beach, beach —
and standing upright — a forest of thighs.

Legs, fascinating creation,
floors in a building — a pile of logs.
Melting, as in hell.
The world in its three thousandth year,

Cards, hands, scraps of skin
how can I find you?
In the middle of parasols, like
an under-water star —
8 back-bones — 8 pairs of legs.

Breathtaking pop art!

Beach, beach,
where one works lying down,
      but idles standing up,
makes up, undresses,
where for 10 kopeks you can glimpse the future —
"From the horizon of one — to the horizon of many..."
"Excuse me, didn't you see my foot? Size 37...
They changed..."

"And then suddenly it looked up —
and soared into the clouds.
A pair of little wings on it,
like garters!
Except, to be more precise: Number 38½!"

The horizons dissolved
between the sky and the water,

the clouds and the islands,
between the stones and my hand.

On the mattress — five girls,
their faces close together,
like the five toes in a girl's sandal,
braided together.

The beach and noon — prolongation
of your divine tread.
Time moves on.
They move on.

I love to enter the aureole of light
where there are no boundaries.
Sea — a half state
between sky and land,
between water and dry-land,
between the many and me,
between fiction and reality,
between soul and substance.

What if in a saturated solution
something else appeared:
dry land, dissolving in the sea,
transformed into the firmament.

And then out of the firmament
something came back to us,
like god and nature
and walking on the water.

It is understood — god was invisible.
Only, a triangular seagull
          motionless in the centre of the sky,
white and breathing heavily —
          like the white bikini of god.

BOAT ON THE SHORE

Over the up-turned boat, at night,
over its aluminium bottom, the tense body
of a gymnast, tortuous back-bone,
shaped like the handle of a steam iron!

In the radiance of the sea, north-amberish,
soldered to the bottom, guffaws a breath,
a teaser, a half-breed, a centaur,
oh, half a boat and half a child...

Half-sea, half-city,
in it a half half-crazy reckoning,
half yearns — half caresses,
half drowns — half rescues.

Suddenly, precipitately she turns over.
Half wild, she slips away — returns,
sinking her toes into the sand ...
But I'll get you yet, my living iron!

IN THE MOUNTAINS

Here, as one breathes, one writes —
Free, and with full heart —
As the heavens blaze
And as the ploughed land rings.

I am giddy from the heights,
And from the highway, blinking
In the sun, the road workers stand
Like half-naked Gods.

And the girls with cherries
And whild berries in their hands —
Like simple Grecian
Goddesses and Bacchantes.

In the sun their noses are peeling,
Like the painting in frescoes.
Here as one loves — one writes —
Boldly, with deep emotion.

THE FIRST ICE

A girl is freezing in the telephone
Booth. In her shabby coat
She hides her face, stained
With tears and lipstick,
Blows on her thin hands.
Her fingers are icicles. In her ears — ear-rings.

She will go back — alone, alone,
The long length of the icy street.
The first ice. This is the first time.
The first glaze of telephone phrases.
A frozen track glitters on her cheeks.
The first ice of injury.

ARROW IN THE WALL

A Tambov wolf is your comrade
and friend
When you tear from the wall
the Punjab bow.

The arm pulls back from the shoulder,
like measuring cloth in GUM.
The arrow starts breathing, insatiable,
like the prolongation of a nipple.

With what fierce femininity
The arrow is driven into the wall —
into the walls and comfort of others.
You can feel a woman in it!

An arrow — in the skeleton building,
in everything that has power and price.
Did you think this is a century of electronics?
It is an arrow in the wall!

Power and fortunes are burning!
An arrow in the wall.
When you are alone, alone
You won't hold back your tears.

Over beautified niches,
dark doubly dark.
The ultimate in beggarliness
there is an arrow in the wall!

Checkmate, blonde bitch!
And I shall say:
"You an Olympian!" and think
of the play of dimples on your belly.

"Aggressor," I shall add, "Scythian..."
And you will say: "To hell with you..."

*

Give me a raw bow-string,
the most silent of arrows,
so quiet, so incredible, as if
a secret angel fled away.

With people, we hardly know each other,
but this has gone on for years.
And beneath my tall house
dark waters flow.

A deep stream of love.
A bright stream of sorrow.
A high wall of forgiveness.
And a clear arrow of pain.

MONOLOGUE WITH COMMENTARY
to Robert Lowell

May
you rest in peace,
        enlightened President.
I'll understand a lot,
if I sit up all night.

I shall take off my cap, and
"Peace" I'll say "to everyone".

Peace to your snoring
        Great Ocean.
Peace to the ploughman in Klin.
Peace
to the Temple of San Francisco,
the floors of which, like breath
        well-proportioned, airy,
may sigh for me just once,
        like their country's lungs...

Peace
to your prick,
Central Park at night,
dense, like instinct,
        like the smell of murder,
you lie at ease
        between huge stone legs —
what are you up to?

Peace
to your banquet,
earthly paradise,
peace to your right
to quarter me,
Peace to the Sun itself,
        which chases darkness away, transforms the map,
(peace to my heart
and millions of sun sicknesses).
History, you are a moan
        of crucified prophets,

(they will descend from their crosses —
        to burn the heretics).

Peace, makers of the new,
dazed to stupefaction!
(Peace, palaces washed clean
by the "cultural revolution" of Florence!)
Decay is raving.
But still, vivat!
The profession of "giving birth"
is more ancient than that of "killing"!
Babies in the midwives' hands
        are squealing,
like megaphones
into hushed ages!

Peace to you,
Hugo,
Millers' dog,
        dear fellow,
You are not a dachshund. You are a shoe,
a moccasin with a sole
that came off.

Somebody Unknown put you
on his left foot
and shuffles along the parquet.
Sometimes He sits in his chair with his legs crossed,
and you stand with your toe
        pointed 45 degrees,
and to everyone you seem to be begging
        for something
from the table.

Ah, Hugo, Hugo... I am also
        somebody's shoe. I feel Something put me on...
Peace to the Unknown,
which does not exist,
and — does...

Peace to the good sailing ship
which opened up America!

I made my Russian words
known to America.

In fighting woods
I yelled for the first time,
breaking off at a high note,
the music of Russia!

Not my throat hurt — but my heart.
America, you are a rhythm.
Peace to my brother
who will follow this path.

The past, like a bell,
beats against the vault of wrong.
Though it hurts — it rings out...

My dear Robert Lowell,
peace to Your letter,
so sad it makes me weep,
I'll cry all day
and be sick of everything —
why play with the game of fists
                (Is this one empty, or that?)
Why learn what a fool is like —
                simple or well-read?

I look into now: it
is older than old times.
Phlegon's buffoonery
is dirtier than filth.

Such a lot of filth everywhere —
but you must believe in pearls!
The soul is a jail, or prison —
but you must sing like a boy!

Peace to your gloom.
That's what you are a poet for;
receiving darkness
you radiate light!

You want peace for everyone.
But it never reaches you.

It's so dark, where are you going,
my poor airplane?

Sleep, sweetheart,
breathe
deeply and evenly.
May your tortured soul
rest in peace,
the little town sparkling on the river
is growing smaller, —
like the dear little strap
of the watch on your wrist, —

so,
        you forgot to take it off again.
It shines and ticks away.
I'll take it off very carefully,
            not to interrupt your breathing, wind it,
and put it to the left, groping,
where the bedside table must be...

        * * *

San Francisco is Kolomenskoye.
This is light in the middle of a hill.
Height, cold like a gulp of water
from a well.

I love you, San Francisco,
Membranous frontispieces,
heights spilling over,
evaporate above me.

In the evening the soaring cubes
are filled with gold —
like transparent smokers
inhaling dangerous red smoke.

This is, cut out of skies
and pinned to bridges,

remorse for betrayal
of my youthful dreams.

My architectural youth,
let me light a cigarette with your fire,
compressing my lips
pale with love.

Before the hotel, like foot-wear,
limousines stand black in line
as if angels have flown away
leaving their galoshes behind ..

We are not angels,
The elegant official
slapped on my visa and did not care...
Sigh for me, San Francisco,
You, Kolomenskoye, sigh.

IRONICAL ELEGY, COMPOSED IN THOSE TERRIBLY SAD MOMENTS WHEN I CANNOT WRITE

A crisis is on me. My soul is mute.
"Not a day without a line," my friend exults.
While I am dumb —
with neither days, nor lines.

My fields lie in a far distant place.
The lights of my factories are blacked out.
And in a dreadful fit of yawning
The faces of my unemployed gape open.

And my critical opponent in an article
writes that I, having turned against everyone,
alone, in the most crisis-less of systems,
am passing through a crisis.

My friend, my northern, my incorruptible friend.
The suit is fine, but it doesn't fit me.
Inside and all around me everything is clear —
but the song won't come.

My taste is degenerating
in the shock of sincere crisis —
I stagger
all crisis, all sincere.

I have become degraded in love.
In the tavern with my guitar, seek friends.
You, you are not degraded —
I have become degraded.

My verse was strong, like sugar cubes.
It whistled like a hockey attack.
I have unlearned the art of rhymes.
My efforts fail.

A strange bird from afar
cries out in sorrow from its lonely flights.
The cranes can weep in chorus.
But the swan has no chorus.

About what, oh my grey one, are you
moaning in the wind to Vladimir the White?
Since the melody is lost, I cannot find the notes.
I am in degradation.

Seven volumes of poetry
are published in our country every day.
While I from friends, from cities
flee like a crazy bitch.

In the forests grown cold
and the dawns grown dumb,
where the spring has become degraded
in the secret solstice of summer...

POEM

From us, like appendicitis,
They extracted shame.

Shamelessness — that is our destiny.
Death we can defy.
But who among us has not blushed?
We have forgotten how to blush.

Through the thickness of our cheek
Light does not penetrate.
But night — like stitches,
brings — no peace.

I think that God
instead of eyes and ears
gave us the membranes of the cheek
like a touch of the soul.

My misfortunes burn,
two organs of shame —
not only for shaving
not only for beating!

I descend to whoever is there.
Confused, I look around —
shame presses my cheek
with the wrong side of an iron.

How shamefully we keep silent,
how slowly we go forward,
I'm ashamed of my scribbling,
even of the spelling.

My distant angel,
I am ashamed of your love
by registered air mail...
I am ashamed for you,

For the tears you shed.
But a thousand times more ashamed
that you will not find tears
in the depths of my soul.

I am a ridiculous person
with swollen, stormy eyes.
It is doubly shameful to cry
Thus for the first time!

And the black stream
slips away on the telephone
for all, for all, which it
had and could not save.

For all, for all, for all
that was and passed on,
that was harnessed
and even so — not all...

In the hospital the director
becomes black with the bed-sheets.
Palms out-stretched.
But a thousand times more shameful

That we are looked at in the eye,
as if we were foreigners,
the diffident beauty
of some cut-glass country.

The bashful reproach
of bashful meadows
of the bashful quivering
of a bashful grove...

The duty of poetry
is to be the organ of shame.

DECEMBER PASTURES

All's well — a crush of stars.
Shepherds in a circle round the fire.
A one-year-old wolf-bitch
is delivering on the snow.

It smells of dog and the New Testament.
How she suffered among us —
her belly sparkling with light,
like a silver porcupine.

The shepherds were playing cards —
kings, kings, kings.
From icons, as from kennels, barking —
dogs, dogs, dogs!
"Arf, arf, Madonna
            Alleluia,
                    may your puppies bless them..."

And she lay down
on burs and dry droppings
and sniffed her shining
strange messianic belly.

Black sheep followed closely.
Only a silver one understood everything.
His silhouette resembled
a bicycle chain.

Somebody riding in the crowd of sheep,
peddling away,
thought: "The Son of Man has not saved them,
let the child of the dog save them..."

It was breathing softly, a blonde puppy,
near three grey ones.
A nimbus, turning over the brow
like a small gear, grew cold.

And from that small gear
started a ten fold
madness of stars and fleas.
For everything that lives is God.

"Apollos", marches, countries,
the course of history and centuries,
Ionian sheep,
ironic snows.

Through the snow, answering hopes,
registered in truck-drivers' taverns,
Herod, dog-catcher, came with a sack
and an apologetic giggle.

ACKNOWLEDGEMENT

Some of these translations have appeared over the years in *Time*, *Prism*, *The Malahat Review*, *Canadian Forum* and *The Tamarack Review*.

I also wish to acknowledge Ryerson Press, McClelland and Stewart, and Hounslow Press.